Animal Detectives

Search for the Facts

SHARKS

Anne O'Daly

Raintree is an imprint of Capstone Global Library Limited, a company incorporated in England and Wales having its registered office at 264 Banbury Road, Oxford, OX2 7DY – Registered company number: 6695582

www.raintree.co.uk
myorders@raintree.co.uk

© Brown Bear Books Limited 2021
Ths edition published by Raintree in 2021

All rights reserved. No part of this publication may be reproduced in any form or by any means (including photocopying or storing it in any medium by electronic means and whether or not transiently or incidentally to some other use of this publication) without the written permission of the copyright owner, except in accordance with the provisions of the Copyright, Designs and Patents Act 1988 or under the terms of a licence issued by the Copyright Licensing Agency, Saffron House, 6–10 Kirby Street, London EC1N 8TS (www.cla.co.uk). Applications for the copyright owner's written permission should be addressed to the publisher.

Created by Brown Bear Books Ltd
Design Manager: Keith Davis
Children's Publisher: Anne O'Daly
Picture Manager: Sophie Mortimer
Printed and bound in India

ISBN 978 1 4747 9847 1 (hardback)
ISBN 978 1 4747 9853 2 (paperback)

London Borough of Enfield	
91200000715858	
Askews & Holts	26-Mar-2021
J597.3 JUNIOR NON-FI	
ENHIGH	

British Library Cataloguing in Publication Data
A full catalogue record for this book is available from the British Library.

Picture Credits
Cover: iStock: Lindsay Imagery; Interior: iStock: Howard Chen 4-5b, Divepic 20, Durden Images 18, Peter Nile 8; Shutterstock: Luis Miguel Estevez 12, Havoc 4bl, 6, Frantisek Hojdysz 5r, 11, JimCatlinPhotography.com 4l, Aleksei Lazukov 5br, Lindsay Lu 14, Fata Morgana by Andrew Marriott 4-5c, mycteria 5tr (inset), Martin Prochazkacz, 5tr, 16, widestanimal 5tl.
t=top, r=right, l=left, c=centre, b=bottom
All artwork and other photography Brown Bear Books.

Every effort has been made to contact copyright holders of material reproduced in this book. Any omissions will be rectified in subsequent printings if notice is given to the publisher.

All the internet addresses (URLs) given in this book were valid at the time of going to press. However, due to the dynamic nature of the internet, some addresses may have changed, or sites may have changed or ceased to exist since publication. While the author and publisher regret any inconvenience this may cause readers, no responsibility for any such changes can be accepted by either the author or the publisher.

Contents

 Sharks

Meet the family 4

Animal files
    Bull shark 6
    Great white shark 8
    Hammerhead 10
    Angel shark 12
    Whale shark 14
    Basking shark 16
    Nurse shark 18
    Tiger shark 20

Quiz 22

Glossary 23

Find out more 23

Index 24

Meet the family

Sharks are fish. They live in the oceans.
Many sharks are deadly hunters.
Others are gentle giants.
Read on to find out more!

Nurse shark

Whale shark

Bull shark

Tiger shark

Sharks

Great white shark

Basking shark

The hammerhead shark has an unusual head. Its shape helps it to find food.

Hammerhead shark

Angel shark

Bull shark

The bull shark is one of most dangerous sharks. It swims in oceans and in rivers. It eats almost anything – even other sharks!

FACT FILE

Scientific name: *Carcharhinus leucas*

Food: turtles, prawns, lobsters, sea urchins, squid, octopus

Habitat: near the coast in warm oceans

The shark's mouth has rows of jagged teeth.

tail

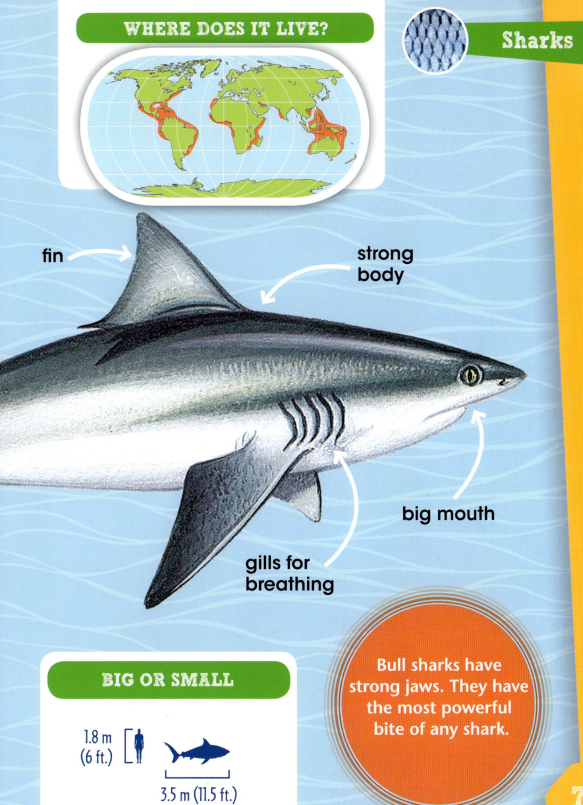

WHERE DOES IT LIVE?

Sharks

- fin
- strong body
- big mouth
- gills for breathing

BIG OR SMALL

1.8 m (6 ft.)
3.5 m (11.5 ft.)

Bull sharks have strong jaws. They have the most powerful bite of any shark.

Great white shark

The great white is a hunting machine!
It speeds through the water.
It catches prey with a huge bite.

FACT FILE

Scientific name: *Carcharodon carcharias*

Food: turtles, seabirds, dolphins, seals, and sea lions, fish including other sharks

Habitat: coastal waters in oceans around the world

Great whites have between 12,000 and 30,000 teeth in their lifetime.

tail

Sharks

WHERE DOES IT LIVE?

torpedo-shaped body

fin

gills

sharp, saw-like teeth

grey and white skin

BIG OR SMALL

1.8 m (6 ft.)

6 m (20 ft.)

Great whites have super senses. A great white can smell blood in the ocean from 5 kilometres (3 miles)!

Hammerhead

This shark has an eye at each end of its head. It can see both sides at once! It looks for food on the seabed.

FACT FILE

Scientific name: *Sphyrnidae*

Food: squid, shellfish, sea snakes, skates, stingrays, other sharks

Habitat: warm oceans, shallow waters around coral reefs

tail

fin

head shaped like a hammer

Eye

Hammerheads give birth to live babies. The baby sharks are called pups.

WHERE DOES IT LIVE?

Sharks

strong body

Hammerheads have white bellies. That makes them harder to see from below.

BIG OR SMALL

1.8 m (6 ft.)

90 cm (3 ft.) to 6 m (20 ft.)

Angel shark

Angel sharks lie on the seabed. They hide in the sand. They wait for prey to swim by. Then they grab it!

FACT FILE

Scientific name: *Squatina squatina*

Food: flatfish, rays, skates, crabs, lobsters and squid

Habitat: in mud and sand on the seabed

tail

This angel shark is buried in the sand. Can you see it?

WHERE DOES IT LIVE?

 Sharks

- fin shaped like a wing
- flat body
- colours match the seabed

BIG OR SMALL

1.8 m (6 ft.)

up to 2.4 m (8 ft.)

Angel sharks have whiskers near their snout. The whiskers help the sharks find food.

13

Whale shark

The whale shark is the biggest fish in the world. Its huge mouth has 3,000 tiny teeth. But it doesn't use them to eat. It sucks in food through its gills.

FACT FILE

Scientific name: *Rhincodon typus*

Food: plankton (tiny plants and animals), small fish, shrimp and other small animals

Habitat: warm waters in the Atlantic, Indian and Pacific Oceans

fin

A diver looks tiny next to this enormous whale shark.

WHERE DOES IT LIVE?

Sharks

grey back with spots and stripes

massive head

large mouth with tiny teeth

body like a whale's

BIG OR SMALL

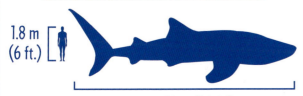

1.8 m (6 ft.)

up to 12 m (40 ft.)

These giants have a long life span. They can live for 70 to 100 years.

15

Basking shark

The basking shark is the second biggest shark. It swims with its huge mouth wide open. It eats tiny creatures in the water.

FACT FILE

Scientific name: *Cetorhinus maximus*

Food: plankton (tiny sea creatures)

Habitat: mainly in cold and cool waters around the world

tail

The shark gulps 6,000 litres (1,500 gallons) of water each hour.

WHERE DOES IT LIVE?

Sharks

small eye

gills

pointed snout

huge jaws, up to 1 m (3 ft.) wide

Basking sharks have babies every two to four years. The babies grow in their mother's body for up to three years.

BIG OR SMALL

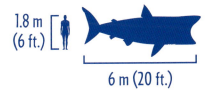

1.8 m (6 ft.)

6 m (20 ft.)

17

Nurse shark

Nurse sharks are gentle giants. But watch out! They can bite. These sharks hunt at night. They spend the day resting on the seafloor.

FACT FILE

Scientific name: *Ginglymostoma cirratum*

Food: fish, crabs, lobsters, stingrays, octupuses and even sea snakes

Habitat: Shallow waters, often near coral reefs

Nurse sharks are peaceful sharks. They are usually harmless to people.

tail

WHERE DOES IT LIVE?

Sharks

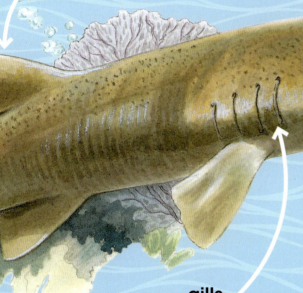

- fin
- small eye
- fleshy whiskers to find food
- gills

BIG OR SMALL

1.8 m (6 ft.)
4.3 m (14 ft.)

Nurse sharks suck up their prey. They make a loud slurp when they eat!

Tiger shark

The tiger shark is a fierce hunter. It has strong jaws and sharp teeth. This shark will attack almost anything!

FACT FILE

Scientific name: *Galeocerdo cuvier*

Food: Fish, turtles, sea snakes, seals, sea lions, whales and dolphins

Habitat: warm water out in the ocean and near the coast

sharp, jagged teeth

white belly

Tiger sharks are named after the black stripes on their back.

WHERE DOES IT LIVE?

Sharks

- large eye
- fin
- dark grey back
- tail
- strong body

BIG OR SMALL

1.8 m (6 ft.)
up to 4.3 m (14 ft)

Tiger sharks are swimming rubbish bins. They will eat bottles, tin cans, rubber tyres and explosives!

Quiz

Test your skills! Can you answer these questions? Look in the book for clues. The answers are on page 24.

2 What does a basking shark eat?

1 How does the angel shark catch its food?

3 How does the tiger shark get its name?

4 How many teeth does a whale shark have?

Glossary

Sharks

fin
Part of a shark's body that helps it swim.

gill
Part of a shark's body that lets it breathe under the water.

habitat
The kind of place where an animal usually lives.

jagged
A sharp, zigzag shape.

life span
How long an animal lives.

prey
An animal that is hunted by another animal for food.

snout
The mouth, nose and jaws.

Find out more

Books

Sharks (Go! Field Guide), Scholastic (Scholastic, 2019)

Sharks and Other Deadly Ocean Creatures: Visual Encyclopedia, DK (DK Children, 2016)

Websites

dkfindout.com/uk/animals-and-nature/fish/sharks/

easyscienceforkids.com/all-about-sharks/

www.ducksters.com/animals/greatwhiteshark.php

Index

baby sharks 10, 17

coast 6, 8, 20

coral reefs 10, 18

fin 7, 8, 10, 13, 14, 18

gills 7, 9, 14, 17, 19

jaws 7, 17, 20

oceans 4, 6, 9, 10, 14, 20

prey 8, 12, 19

seabed 10, 12, 13

senses 9

teeth 6, 8, 9, 14, 15, 20

whiskers 13, 19

Quiz Answers: 1. It hides on the seabed and waits for prey to swim past. **2.** Plankton (tiny sea creatures). **3.** From the black stripes on its back. **4.** It has 3,000 teeth.